# SOUL-LAG™: Realigning Your Life



By

GAURAV PATEL

*"When the pace of life outgrows the rhythm of the soul, alignment becomes survival"*

Clever Fox® PUBLISHING

**Chennai • Bangalore**

CLEVER FOX PUBLISHING
Chennai, India

Published by CLEVER FOX PUBLISHING 2025

ISBN: 978-93-7500-205-5

# CONTENTS

# READER'S GUIDE: HOW TO USE THIS BOOK

## 1. This Book Is a Journey, Not a Manual

You won't find numbered steps or fixed answers here.

**Soul-Lag** is a rhythm — a way of understanding when life moves faster than your soul.

You don't read it once and "finish" it. You move with it. You loop back when you drift.

Let each chapter meet you where you are.

---

## 2. Meet Arnav — and Yourself

The story follows Arnav, a driven professional who represents all of us:

ambitious yet tired, connected yet distant, successful yet restless.

As you follow his journey, you may see your own reflections —

in his work pressure, in his relationships, in his rediscovery of silence.

Don't rush his story.

Observe. Reflect. Let it unfold with your pace.

---

## 3. Notice the Diagrams — They're Maps, Not Theories

Each visual in this book —from The Alignment Loop™ to The Flow Continuum —

is not just a concept but a mirror.

Pause when you reach one.

Ask: Where am I on this map today?

The diagrams are meant to be lived with, not just looked at.

---

## 4. Use the Reflection Boxes

### Every chapter ends with a short reflection box.

---

You don't need to answer all questions at once.

Pick one. Sit with it. Journal if you'd like.

These are not for self-critique; they're for self-connection.

If you give them your attention, they'll give you clarity.

---

## 5. The Workbook at the End Is Your Alignment Practice

After the story, you'll find a section called "Your Realignment Journey."

That's where Arnav's world becomes yours.

It includes practical tools like the Soul-Lag™ Assessment Matrix and the Alignment Loop™ Exercise.

Return to it anytime — when you feel the drift, when you need reflection, or when you want to realign.

---

## 6. Don't Rush the Loop

There will be parts of this book that feel like déjà vu —

awareness, reflection, alignment, and drift.

That's intentional.

Growth is not linear; it's cyclical.

Each loop brings you deeper understanding and softer strength.

Read slowly. Reflect deeply. Return freely.

---

## 7. Let the Book Read You Back

Some books you read.

Others read you.

This one does both.

If you allow it, Soul-Lag will gently show you where your rhythm has broken —

not to shame you, but to guide you back to balance.

Because real alignment isn't found in escape.

It's found in awareness — in the quiet courage to sync again.

---

You don't have to finish this book to begin transformation.

You began the moment you paused to listen.

# PREFACE — WHEN THE SOUL STARTS TO SLOW

There comes a point when even achievement feels heavy.

When success, once electric, begins to hum like static.

When the life you built starts moving faster than the life you can feel.

I call that moment **Soul-Lag.**

It's not burnout, though it may look like it.

It's not depression, though it may feel close.

It's the invisible distance between your outer speed and your inner rhythm —

a quiet signal that something within you is asking to realign.

I first noticed it not in others, but in myself.

Years of chasing outcomes, goals, and milestones had left me accomplished — yet oddly absent.

I could manage teams, strategies, deadlines — but not silence.

The more the world demanded pace, the more I lost peace.

For a long time, I thought slowing down was the answer.

It wasn't.

What helped wasn't stopping — it was syncing.

That's when Soul-Lag took shape — not as a diagnosis, but as a dialogue.

A space where exhaustion softens into awareness, and awareness returns to realignment.

---

## The Birth of an Idea

This book began as late-night notes — quiet reflections after long days when the noise refused to fade.

Each line felt like a breadcrumb pointing to the same truth:

The soul doesn't demand escape from speed; it asks for rhythm within the movement.

I began observing the same drift in everyone around me —

students pressured to excel, parents quietly stretched thin, professionals burning at both ends,

even creators whose passion had quietly turned into a performance.

Different stories, same undertone: life had outpaced their inner rhythm.

That's when the concept of **The Alignment Loop** took shape — not as a productivity hack, but as a way back to your inner timing.

A simple, repeatable rhythm to help close the gap between movement and meaning:

**Recognize → Recenter → Reflect → Realign.**

Every time you move through this loop with intention, the lag softens — and peace begins to flow again.

---

## What This Book Isn't

This is not a self-help manual.

There are no promises of overnight clarity or eternal calm.

Instead, this book is an invitation — to slow down enough to see,

to listen deeply enough to feel, to reflect enough to return.

Through the story of Arnav, you'll experience this journey from exhaustion to awareness, from chaos to coherence.

His story mirrors all of ours' — filled with ambition, conflict, and rediscovery.

As you read, you may realize you don't need to abandon your world to heal.

You simply need to walk beside your soul again.

---

## A Note Before You Begin

If you're here, you've already heard the whisper.

That subtle inner knowing that something needs to shift — not outside, but within.

Let this book be your companion in that shift.

Don't rush it. Don't try to fix yourself.

Just Recognize. Recenter. Reflect. Realign.

Because the moment you recognize your own Soul-Lag™, you've already begun to sync again.

---

When the world moves faster than your soul, don't stop running — **realign your rhythm**.

**– Gaurav Patel**

# AUTHOR'S NOTE

*I* didn't write this book because I had answers.

I wrote it because I had questions that refused to stay quiet.

For years, I lived a version of success everyone recognizes — achievement, ambition, recognition.

But beneath it, there was a silence I couldn't name — a kind of inner delay, as if my soul hadn't caught up with my life.

That delay became my turning point.

I called it **Soul-Lag**.

It began as a private note in a journal and grew into a language — one that helped me, and later many others, make sense of an exhaustion that didn't show up in medical tests or performance reviews.

It wasn't failure.

It was feedback.

This book wasn't born from escape. It was born from a return — to rhythm, to reflection, and to realignment.

A collection of moments, lessons, and frameworks that arrived gradually, as I relearned how to walk beside my own thoughts again.

You'll meet Arnav in these pages — but he isn't just a character.

He is a mirror for anyone who has ever felt behind while doing everything right.

His story carries the tension so many of us live — the pull between outer motion and inner meaning.

If there's one truth this journey has taught me, it's this:

You cannot outrun your soul.

But you can always sync back with it.

So read this book not as a set of instructions, but as an invitation.

Pause where something moves you.

Reflect when it challenges you.

And above all, trust the lag — because it is not a flaw. It is a compass.

**— Gaurav Patel**

*Author of Soul-Lag™: Realigning Your Life*

# PROLOGUE – THE PAUSE BEFORE THE FALL

The city lights flickered like rewards — constant, bright, unblinking.

From the 27th floor, Arnav could see the skyline that once felt like victory.

Tonight, it looked like distance.

The presentation had gone perfectly.

He'd spoken with precision, earned the nods, and closed the deal.

But as applause filled the room, all he felt was a peculiar quiet — as if his soul hadn't attended the meeting.

It wasn't sadness.

It wasn't failure.

It was delay — a soft, widening gap between how fast life was moving and how slowly he was catching up.

At first, he called it fatigue.

He tried the usual fixes — a weekend off, a productivity podcast, and a meditation app.

Each brought calm for a moment, but every Monday morning, the rush returned and swallowed him again.

And somewhere between one task and the next, the gap grew.

More success, less meaning.

More speed, less soul.

Arnav didn't know it then, but he was living what millions silently endure — when achievement outruns awareness, and the soul begins to lag behind.

He would later learn that Soul-Lag wasn't a breakdown — it was a message.

A pause before evolution.

A quiet signal that the next chapter of life would no longer be about speed —

but about sync.

CHAPTER 1

# THE BREAKING POINT

The day after the presentation, the office looked the same, but something inside Arnav had shifted.

The noise felt louder now — keyboards clacking, phones vibrating, and the low hum of ambition in motion.

He watched his team debate over slide decks, arguing about fonts and deadlines as though perfection could save them.

He remembered doing the same — until the applause in that glass room turned hollow in his ears.

He'd crossed an invisible line — not between failure and success, but between drive and drain.

He spent the rest of the morning pretending. Pretending to focus. Pretending to care. Pretending he was fine. His jaw clenched without him noticing.

At lunch, he skipped the cafeteria and drove aimlessly. His fingers tightened around the steering wheel — not in anger but in a quiet kind of fatigue.

The car radio played another "how-to-be-your-best-self" podcast — the same voice urging him to optimize, strategize, and maximize.

He switched it off halfway through. Silence filled the car — thick, unfamiliar, and strangely kind.

For the first time in months, he didn't want advice.

He wanted space.

---

## Scene – A Quiet Coffee Shop

He found himself in a corner café he used to visit years ago, before everything was scheduled so tightly.

The smell of roasted beans and rain on the pavement pulled something loose inside him.

The barista looked up: "Your usual?"

He hesitated.

"I'm not sure what that is anymore."

She smiled, assuming he meant the drink.

But he knew he wasn't talking about coffee.

When he picked up the cup, his hand wasn't shaking, but there was a tremor somewhere beneath the skin — a silent, restless pulse.

He took a seat by the window and opened his notebook.

Blank pages stared back — pages that once overflowed with ideas, sketches, and hopes.

Now, they stood as silent witnesses to a man too busy to hear his own thoughts.

He scribbled a sentence:

**"I don't know who's running faster — me or the world."**

Another line followed, soft but steady:

**"Maybe the lag isn't the enemy."**

He didn't fully understand it.

But truth often arrives disguised as confusion — steady, persistent, and impossible to ignore.

---

## The Diagnosis No Doctor Gives

That evening, his wife Meera looked up from her laptop. "You're home early."

He nodded, dropped his bag, and sank into the couch — his ribcage straining for a slow, steady breath.

"Rough day?" she asked.

"Not really," he said. "Just… noisy."

She tilted her head.

"Outside or inside?"

He gave a tired smile.

"Both."

Silence settled — warm, unforced.

No fixing. No advice. Just presence.

He realized that's what he had been missing — stillness without an agenda.

Every other form of calm had been a task: ten minutes of meditation, five steps to focus, and three ways to relax.

Peace that is scheduled isn't peace.

It's performance.

He whispered, "Maybe what I'm feeling isn't burnout. Maybe it's Soul-Lag."

Meera looked at him curiously. "Soul-what?"

He laughed under his breath. "I don't know. But it just feels right."

---

## The Moment of Naming

Naming it changed something.

Chaos turned into language.

Language turned into understanding.

Soul-Lag wasn't failure — it was feedback.

Pilots, he'd later read, trust instruments over instinct when disoriented.

Maybe life worked the same way.

Maybe the lag wasn't a crack — but a signal.

Not to scare him. But to guide him back.

**Soul-Lag™ Insight:**

***Awareness is the compass that appears when control disappears.***

He leaned back, closed his eyes, and letting the city hum dissolve into the background music.

Every sound — the horns, chatter, and clinking cups — felt like rhythm returning.

He didn't need a plan yet,

Just presence.

---

## Reflection Box – Pause & Realign

- Where am I confusing motion with progress?
- When was the last time I sat in silence without reaching for a solution?
- What if discomfort is just my inner self asking me to slow enough to listen?

**Soul-Lag™ Insight:**

***You can't outpace your soul.***

***But you can learn to move with it.***

---

## Closing Scene

That night, Arnav picked up his notebook again. He wrote three lines:

1. The lag means I'm alive.
2. Awareness is arrival.
3. Tomorrow, I will start **realigning**.

He didn't know what realignment would look like yet.

But for the first time in a long time, he felt a quiet confidence — the kind that doesn't come from winning, but from waking up.

Outside, the city kept rushing. Inside, he finally stopped running.

And in that stillness, the journey truly began.

---

## Diagram 1 / Chapter 1

*Soul-Lag™ Curve*

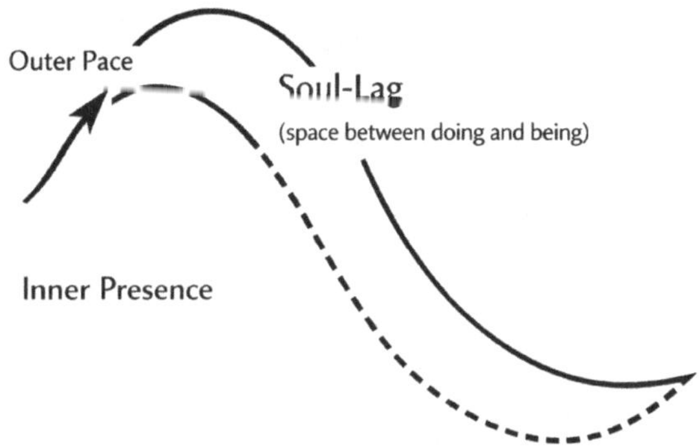




---

*"Pace outruns presence.*
*Awareness brings us home."*
**– Soul-Lag™ Principle**

---

### Author's Note

*When action runs ahead of alignment, performance, culture, and decision-quality decline.*

*Closing the lag restores clarity, resilience, and meaningful progress.*

CHAPTER 2

# THE NOISE WITHIN

## Opening Scene

The city woke before the sun.

Horns, alerts, headlines, and half-read messages flooded the morning like static.

Arnav's phone vibrated against the nightstand — calendar reminders, team pings, and yet another podcast promising "Five Steps to a Perfect Mindset."

He listened anyway.

The host spoke about balance, dopamine, and morning rituals.

For a few minutes, it sounded profound — until the ad break reminded him that peace now came with a premium membership.

He smiled wryly.

Even calm had a subscription.

---

## The Search for Instant Relief

Over months he had collected solutions like trophies:

- Breath-work timers
- Productivity apps
- Gratitude journals with prompts
- A therapist whose calm voice soothed him for forty-eight hours at a time

Each gave him temporary stillness, like switching the wallpaper of his mind.

But fatigue always returned — quiet, familiar, loyal.

*The world sold shortcuts to serenity, he thought, and he had bought every one.*

He realized he had become addicted to improvement itself — chasing better versions while forgetting the one that simply was.

---

## The Commute of Echoes

On the metro, he saw faces lit by blue screens. Everyone scrolling, everyone escaping.

An announcement crackled overhead; nobody listened.

He saw himself in that reflection — head bowed, fingers twitching, thoughts racing faster than the train.

He remembered the boy he used to be — the one who could sit on a rooftop for hours just watching clouds drift.

That memory hurt in a tender way.

Where did that stillness go?

---

## The Silent Diagnosis

At lunch, he met his friend Rishi, who had recently discovered meditation.

"You should try it," Rishi said. "Ten minutes a day changed my life."

Arnav nodded politely. "And then what?"

Rishi blinked. "Then I just… feel lighter."

Arnav smiled. "Until the next meeting?"

They laughed, but both knew the truth: the peace was borrowed, not earned.

That night, staring at the ceiling fan, Arnav realized therapy, podcasts, and mindfulness apps had given him knowledge — but not wisdom.

He was informed, not transformed.

---

## The Moment of Recognition

At 2 a.m., he finally wrote in his notebook:

"Every quick fix delays the real fix."

"Maybe the goal isn't quieting the noise — but understanding it."

He felt something loosen — like a knot he'd stopped pulling against.

Awareness entered softly, without drama.

---

### Reflection Box – Pause & Realign

- Which "instant comforts" do I reach for when discomfort knocks?
- What pattern do I repeat that brings only temporary relief?
- If I stopped fixing for a moment, what truth might appear?

**Soul-Lag™ Insight:**

***Awareness doesn't silence the noise. It teaches you to hear the music beneath it.***

---

### Closing Scene

Morning light slipped through half-drawn curtains.

Meera stirred beside him. The city outside was already racing, but for once he didn't rush to join it.

He lay still, breathing with the rhythm of dawn.

No playlists, no podcasts — just heartbeat and air.

He didn't call it meditation. He called it listening.

And somewhere inside that listening, he could almost feel the gears of life realigning—quietly, mercifully, at last.

---

**Diagram 2 / Chapter 2**

## THE SURFACE RELIEF LOOP

— How Quick Fixes Keep Us Stuck —

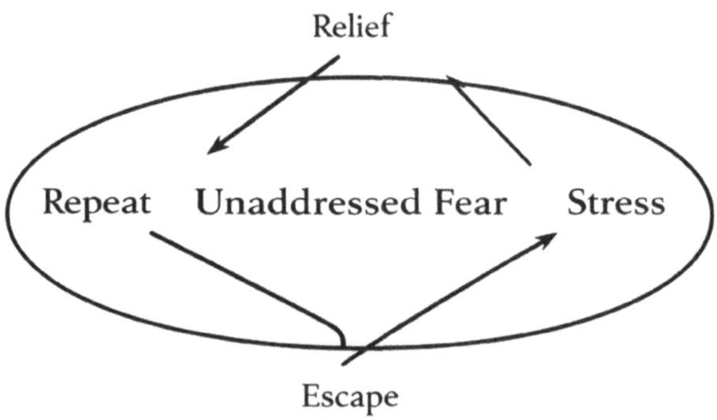


Surface fixes: Scrolling · Motivation clips · Micro-meditation bursts



---

*"We escape for comfort. We return for growth."*

**– Soul-Lag™ Principle**

---

## Author's Note

*Short-term relief helps us cope. Returning to our inner clarity helps us grow.*

*Leaders rise not by avoiding fear, but by turning towards it and acting from alignment.*

CHAPTER 3

# ECHOES OF A SMALL TOWN

## The Return

The train slowed as it entered the small station.

A single chai stall, a rusted clock, and the faint smell of wet soil greeted Arnav like an old melody.

After years of airports and lounges, the quiet almost startled him.

He had come home after his father's minor surgery, but somewhere deeper, he knew this trip wasn't about recovery — it was about remembrance.

The house looked smaller, the ceilings lower, yet the silence larger than he remembered.

His father sat repairing a table fan, humming softly, the screwdriver tapping in rhythm.

It was the same sound Arnav once found irritating — the slow, methodical pace of someone with time.

Now it sounded like peace.

---

### The Mirror of Origins

Over dinner, his mother asked, "You still eat fast."

He smiled. "Occupational hazard."

He caught himself glancing at his phone even though he had no notifications here.

The habit moved faster than thought.

She shook her head. "You were born impatient. Even as a child, you couldn't wait for laddoos to cool."

They laughed, but the words lingered.

Maybe impatience wasn't new — maybe he had simply industrialized it.

From childhood, life had been a race to arrive somewhere better.

Better grades, better college, better job — until "better" became endless.

That night, lying on the old cot, he listened to crickets and ceiling fans.

There were no horns, no notifications, no deadlines — only rhythm.

He realized: the world here still moved at the pace of breath.

---

## Flashback — The Scholarship

He remembered the day his father sold his gold watch to pay his first-year hostel fee.

“Don’t waste this time, Arnav,” he’d said.

Back then, Arnav had heard pressure.

Now he heard love.

But love misheard can become performance.

He’d spent his youth proving he was worth the sacrifice.

Somewhere along the line, gratitude turned into obligation, and obligation became speed.

**Soul-Lag™ Insight:**

***Realignment often begins by forgiving the version of yourself who thought survival required speed.***

---

## The Conversation

“Papa,” he said the next morning, “did you ever feel left behind?”

His father looked up from the newspaper.

“Left behind? No. Sometimes just… left alone.”

"What do you mean?"

His father folded the paper.

"When everyone runs, silence becomes company. If you can stay with it, you win differently."

The line landed like a seed.

His chest tightened — not painfully, just enough to remind him that ambition had always lived close to fear.

Maybe Soul-Lag wasn't a gap to close — maybe it was the space to hear what stillness was saying.

---

### Reflection Box – Pause & Realign

- Which childhood message still drives my definition of "enough"?
- Am I running toward success or away from fear?
- What would slowing down feel like if it wasn't called failure?

## Closing Scene

As Arnav packed to leave, his father handed him the repaired fan.

"It works now," he said. "Just needed a little oil."

Arnav smiled. "Maybe I did too."

On the train back, he watched fields blur past the window.

For the first time, he didn't feel torn between two worlds.

He felt both moving inside him — one teaching ambition, the other reminding him of rhythm.

He wrote in his notebook:

"Awareness doesn't erase the past.

It tunes it until it hums in harmony."

The whistle blew, and the city pulled him forward again — not faster, just clearer.

**"Silence soothed him, but it also revealed how noisy he had become inside."**

---

## Diagram 3 / Chapter 3

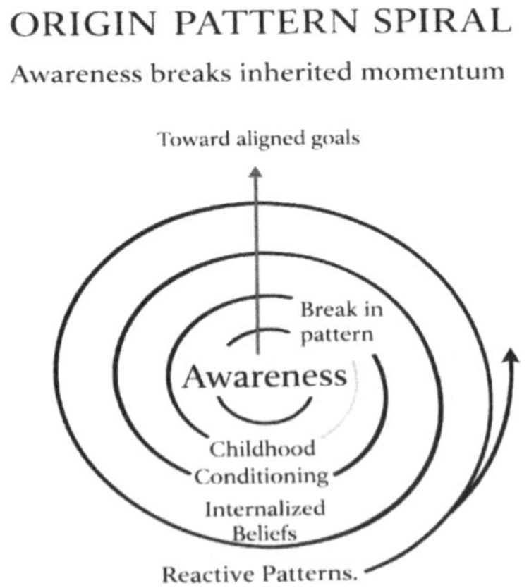

---

*"Awareness softens the speed we inherited as survival "*

**– Soul-Lag™ Principle**

---

**Author's Note**

*Patterns repeat until presence interrupts them. The moment we notice , we are no longer inside it – we are above it.*

*And that shift is where real freedom begins.*

CHAPTER 4

# LESSONS IN SILENCE

## The Weight of Sound

The office cafeteria buzzed with overlapping voices, espresso machines, and the polite chaos of modern survival.

Arnav sat alone, stirring his coffee long after it had gone cold.

He wasn't escaping work; he was observing it.

His knee bounced under the table before he noticed — his body trying to outrun his mind again.

Every conversation carried an undertone of urgency — deadlines, deliverables, distractions.

He realized that nobody spoke in pauses anymore.

Silence had become impolite.

When he got back to his desk, he opened his inbox, hovered over a dozen unread messages, and did something unthinkable — he closed the laptop.

He leaned back, closed his eyes, and listened: the hum of the air-conditioner, a keyboard somewhere, his own heartbeat.

Beneath all of it, a strange music — a rhythm he hadn't heard in years.

---

## Flashback — The Professor

Memory pulled him back to college.

A communication skills class, of all places.

Professor Dev had said, "Most people listen to reply. The wise listen to understand. But the rarest listen to themselves."

At the time, Arnav thought it was poetic nonsense.

Now it sounded like prophecy.

He remembered how Dev used to pause mid-lecture, letting silence stretch until the room fidgeted.

"See?" he'd say, smiling. "You feel discomfort only because silence holds truth."

---

## The Practice of Listening

That night, Arnav tried something new.

No music, no podcasts, no guided breathing.

Just ten minutes of sitting still.

The first minute was chaos — random thoughts, to-do lists, irritation.

By the fifth, something shifted: the thoughts were still there, but softer, less urgent.

By the tenth, he felt a kind of clarity he couldn't explain — not calm, but space.

He realized silence wasn't empty; it was full — of everything he usually ignored.

**Soul-Lag™ Insight**

***Reflection is the dialogue between awareness and action.***

***Without it, even growth becomes noise.***

---

## The Unexpected Test

The next morning, a crisis hit: a client escalation, angry emails, leadership calls.

For a split second, his breath tightened and the old urge to react flickered — proof that speed still lived inside him.

Instead, he asked for ten minutes before responding.

He went to the terrace, breathed, and watched clouds drift.

When he finally replied, his words were calm, precise — no justification, just a solution.

Within an hour, the issue dissolved.

His teammate whispered later, "What happened to you? You didn't even raise your voice."

Arnav smiled. "I paused."

The old urge to react flickered — but it passed, like weather moving across a calmer sky.

Silence doesn't slow you; it strengthens your signal.

---

### Reflection Box – Pause & Realign

- When was the last time I chose silence over reaction?
- What truth emerges when I stop filling the space?
- How often do I confuse noise with progress?

## Closing Scene

That evening, Meera found him on the balcony again.

No phone, no laptop — just a notebook open to blank pages.

"Writing something?" she asked.

He nodded. "Maybe. Or maybe I'm just listening."

She smiled. "You look different."

"I feel different," he said. "For once, I'm not running ahead of my thoughts. I'm walking beside them."

Below them, the city shimmered in its usual urgency.

But within him, a quieter city had begun to form — one built on rhythm instead of rush.

He didn't know it yet, but this was the third step of **The Alignment Loop™** — reflection finding its way back to realignment.

---

## Diagram 4 / Chapter 4

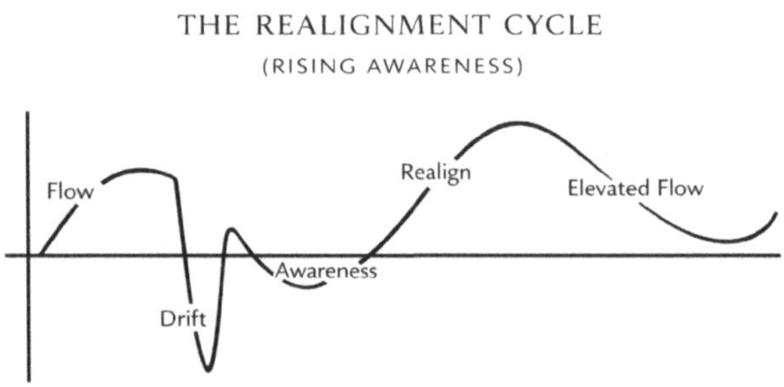




---

*Fall. Notice. Return. Rise.*

**– Soul-Lag™ Principle**

---

## Author's Note

*We all drift. Awareness brings us back.*

*Realignment lifts us higher than where we began.*

*This is how we evolve — cycle by cycle.*

CHAPTER 5

# THE FIRST PAUSE

## The Unexpected Detour

Monday morning.

Arnav was halfway to the airport when his phone buzzed: "*Flight delayed by 3 hours.*"

Three hours once meant lost productivity; today, it felt like borrowed time.

Yet a familiar twitch surfaced — a tiny frustration, a flicker of the old pace.

He exhaled, letting it pass like a wave recede.

He parked near a small café opposite the terminal — a place he'd never noticed before — and ordered tea instead of coffee.

For the first time in months, he had nowhere to be but here.

He took out his notebook.

Yesterday's last line stared back: "*I'm walking beside my thoughts.*"

He smiled. The words didn't feel like an affirmation — they felt like truth.

The city outside moved, but he didn't feel left behind.

His fingers tapped the cup once — muscle memory — then stilled.

---

## A Conversation with Stillness

An elderly traveller sat at the next table.

"Flight delayed?" the man asked.

"Yes," Arnav said.

The old man chuckled. "Then the universe decided you needed to wait."

Arnav laughed. "I used to hate waiting."

"Most do," the man said. "But every pause hides a message.

Only when we stop can life finish its sentence."

The words landed like a stone dropping into still water.

---

## Realization on the Runway

As the announcement finally called passengers to board, Arnav felt no rush.

Still, his feet hesitated for a second — the old urge to race ahead whispered.

He smiled at the instinct and chose to move slowly instead.

By the time he took his seat, he noticed something subtle:

He was not *trying* to relax. He simply was.

The delay had given him what discipline never did — a genuine pause.

He realized stillness isn't scheduled; it's surrendered.

### Soul-Lag™ Insight

***Flow doesn't arrive when you finish everything; it begins when you stop fighting time.***

---

## The Return Home

Later that night, Meera asked, "How was the trip?"

He smiled. "Didn't take it. But I still arrived."

She raised an eyebrow. "At where?"

He tapped his chest. "Here."

She laughed softly. "That's new."

He nodded. "So is peace."

**Reflection Box – Pause & Realign**

- What if waiting isn't wasted time but wisdom time?
- How often do I fill pauses just to feel productive?
- What rhythm appears when I stop chasing moments?

**Soul-Lag™ Insight**

***Flow begins when you honour the gap between doing and being.***

---

## Closing Scene

Arnav wrote before sleeping:

*"Every pause I fear is a path I need.*

*Every delay carries direction.*

*Flow is not motion; it's permission."*

He closed the notebook.

The air-conditioner hummed softly, matching the steady rhythm of his breath.

For the first time in years, he fell asleep without effort.

Outside, the city still raced.

Inside, time exhaled.

---

## Diagram 5 / Chapter 5

### THE FLOW WINDOW

FLOW / PRESENCE

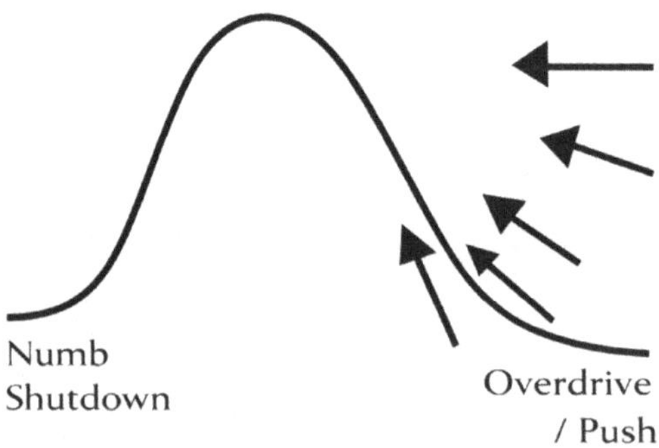


Flow rises between comfort and chaos.



---

*"Flow rises between comfort and chaos."*

**– Soul-Lag™ Principle**

---

**Author's Note**

*Flow happens between disengagement and overdrive —*

*Where challenge energizes and focus stays steady.*

CHAPTER 6

# THE ALIGNMENT LOOP

## The Quiet Blueprint

A week after the delayed flight, Arnav found himself at home on a Sunday morning.

No meetings. No alarms. Just the soft rhythm of rain on the balcony railing.

He opened his notebook — not to record the day, but to understand the pattern forming beneath it.

Each pause, each breath, each moment of returning to himself felt connected.

Not in a line but in a circle.

Growth, he realized, wasn't forward.

It was inward. And then outward again.

He began sketching slowly, letting the inner logic reveal itself:

**Recognize → Recenter → Reflect → Realign**.

He stared at the loop.

It looked simple, almost obvious — but in that simplicity lived everything he had forgotten:

Awareness.

Presence.

Understanding.

Alignment.

He wrote across the top:

**The Alignment Loop™**

Not a hack.

Not a morning routine.

A way of returning — again and again.

---

## The First Test

A few days later, an old colleague blamed him publicly for a project delay.

Old Arnav would have reacted instantly — defended, explained, proved.

His heart still jumped; old habits don't die, they whisper.

But he paused.

He opened his notebook.

He walked himself through the loop:

**Recognize** – *I feel attacked. My ego wants to defend.*

**Recenter** – *A slow breath, shoulders relaxed, grounded in calm.*

**Reflect** – *This isn't personal. He's overwhelmed. I don't need to react to protect my identity.*

**Realign** – *Respond for resolution, not ego.*

He replied with clarity, not defensiveness:

*"Let's revisit the timeline together. We can fix this."*

Within hours, the tension dissolved.

That night he wrote:

**"Alignment is intelligence choosing stillness before movement."**

---

## The Model Revealed

He saw now:

**The Alignment Loop** wasn't a tool to avoid difficulty

It was a way to walk through difficulty **without abandoning yourself**.

Not self-control.

Self-return.

Not productivity.

Presence.

Not linear progress.

**Circular evolution**.

Every time he completed the loop, the gap between reaction and wisdom got smaller.

Not perfect.

Just clearer.

**Why it works**

He wrote a line beneath the diagram:

- **Recognize** – Name the drift.
- **Recenter** – Return to breath, body, truth.
- **Reflect** – See what's real – not what fear says.
- **Realign** – Choose action from clarity, not pressure.

It wasn't a motivational cycle.

It was a nervous system cycle.

A rhythm of awareness and movement.

A way back to himself.

**Soul-Lag™ Insight**

*Awareness without grounding is confusion.*

*Grounding without reflection is escape.*

*Reflection without action is stagnation.*

*Action without awareness is chaos.*

**Alignment is where the four meet.**

---

## Everyday Application

Over the next few weeks, the loop became a quiet companion:

- A disagreement with Meera softened after he paused to recentre, not win.
- A missed target at work became a lesson, not self-judgement.
- An old memory became forgiveness, not friction.

Each time he drifted, he noticed sooner.

Each time he returned, he returned softer and stronger.

He wasn't chasing calm anymore.

He was building it.

Every moment of awareness begins a new loop.

---

### Reflection Box – Pause & Realign

- Where do I drift the most — in recognizing, recentering, reflecting, or realigning?
- How can I make returning to myself a rhythm, not a rescue plan?
- What if growth isn't speed, but steady return?

## Closing Scene

One evening, he met his friend Rishi by the lakeside.

"You seem different," Rishi said.

Arnav smiled. "Not different. Just...aligned."

Rishi laughed. "Is that another framework?"

"Maybe," Arnav said. "But this one breathes."

They watched lights ripple on the water.

The world was still moving fast — emails, deadlines, ambitions.

But he felt no chase inside him.

Life wasn't pulling him.

It was moving with him.

He whispered to himself:

"The world didn't slow down, I simply returned."

And in that gentle return, the loop completed another circle.

---

**Diagram 6 / chapter 6**

*The Alignment Loop™ Model*

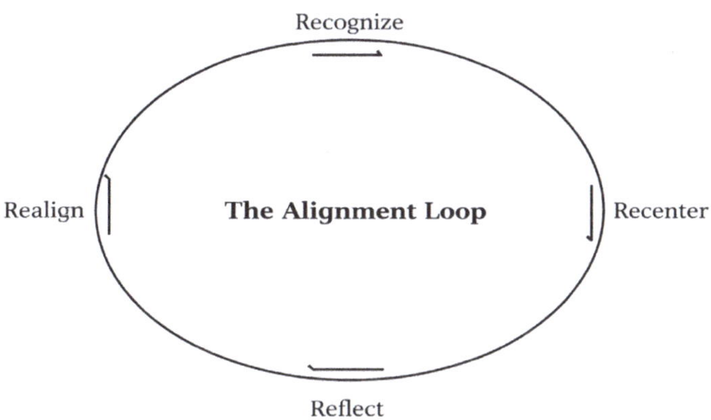




---

*"Alignment isn't reached once — it's returned to, again and again."*

**– Soul-Lag™ Principle**

---

## Author's Note

*The practice isn't to stay aligned, but to return to alignment with greater speed, honesty, and intention each time.*

CHAPTER 7

# THE DRIFT RETURNS

## The Calm After the Calm

For weeks everything worked.

Workdays flowed, evenings felt lighter, even his sleep deepened.

He thought, *maybe I've cracked it.*

But life has a way of testing what you think you've learned.

A global project came in — high stakes, impossible timelines.

His team was stretched; expectations ballooned.

Emails multiplied, meetings blurred, and the old familiar pulse of urgency crept back like background static.

At first, he noticed it.

Then justified it.

Then, quietly, unknowingly, he surrendered to it.

His shoulders tightened without his permission. Coffee cups multiplied on his desk.

The breath that had once been slow and steady became short, rushed, and clipped.

Within a month, reflection had been replaced by reaction again.

**The loop had broken.**

---

## The Subtle Return of Noise

He snapped at Meera for something trivial — the dishes, the door left unlocked.

Her eyebrows lifted in surprise; his heart sank before his words even finished leaving his mouth.

The next morning, he woke up with guilt pressing against his chest like a stalled breath.

He realized he hadn't paused, journaled, or sat in silence in days.

The speed had returned; the soul hadn't caught up.

He had drifted.

But this time, the drift didn't feel like failure — it felt like data.

He could see it happening, like watching himself from a slight distance.

That awareness itself was progress.

---

## Dialogue with Self

That night, he sat alone, notebook open.

The pages from previous weeks were neat and structured; tonight's lines wobbled, uneven — like his breath.

"I'm slipping again."

He paused, fingers tightening around the pen for a moment.

"But maybe slipping is part of the dance."

He wrote until the lines steadied again.

He remembered: growth doesn't erase chaos; it teaches you to return faster.

The drift was not regression — it was rehearsal.

**Soul-Lag™ Insight**

***Realignment isn't about staying in flow;***

***it's about returning to it with grace.***

---

## The Ripple Lesson

During a leadership session, a young analyst froze during her presentation.

Her voice trembled; her hand shook slightly over the clicker.

Old Arnav would have jumped in — filled the silence, fixed it, moved on.

His fingers twitched towards the table — the old reflex to take control.

He noticed. He stayed still.

This time, he took a breath, letting the discomfort hang in the room for just a moment.

"Take a breath," he said gently. "We're not in a hurry."

She inhaled, exhaled, steadied herself, then continued — stronger.

After the meeting she approached him. "You gave me space." She whispered.

Arnav smiled. "Someone gave it to me once too — silence did."

He realized that every time he remembered his own drift, he became more compassionate toward others learning to return.

### Reflection Box – Pause & Realign

- How do I respond when I relapse into old patterns?
- What if progress means noticing the fall sooner, not never falling?
- Where can I build rituals that bring me back to center quickly?

**Soul-Lag™ Insight**

**Mastery isn't eliminating the drift.**

**It's shortening the distance between drift and return.**

---

## Closing Scene

That weekend, he and Meera went for a long drive.

No destination, no playlist. Just road and sky.

Wind poured through the windows like freedom rediscovered.

At one point she asked, "Aren't you supposed to be preparing for that big review?"

He chuckled softly, feeling the question tug at his chest.

The old reflex to justify rose for a moment — then softened.

"This is preparation," he said.

The highway curved, sunlight flickered between passing branches, and for one brief breath, everything aligned — motion, mind, and meaning.

The drift had returned only to remind him of the way home.

He whispered into the breeze,

"It's a rhythm to respect."

And as the car slipped deeper into the horizon, **the loop quietly began again**.

---

## Diagram 7/ Chapter 7

Inner Equilibrium Map
Emotional States Around Awareness

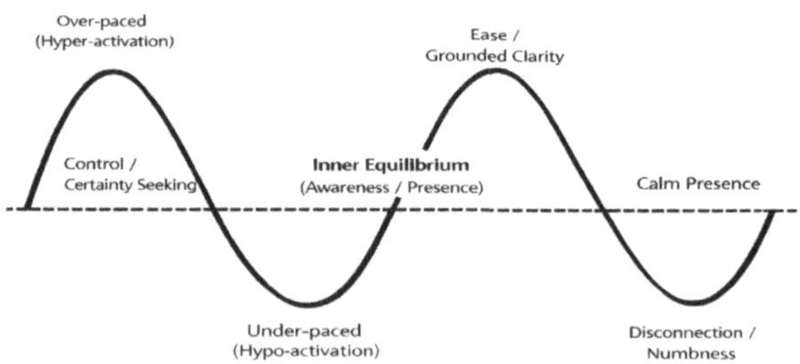




---

*"We drift. We remember. We return.*
*We become."*

**– Soul-Lag™ Principle**

---

## Author's Note

*Moments of disconnection remind us who we are.*

*Returning to awareness is how we evolve into who we are meant to become.*

CHAPTER 8

# RELEARNING FLOW

## The New Rhythm

Arnav woke before dawn.

No alarms, no pressure — just a pale ribbon of morning spilling through the window, slow and deliberate.

He brewed his coffee and sat by the window.

No guided meditation, no playlist, no productivity ritual.

Only breath.

He opened his notebook without a plan.

No prompts, no checklists — just curiosity.

He wrote one line:

**"I am not chasing balance anymore. I'm living rhythm."**

A small smile tugged at his mouth.

Not triumph — recognition.

Balance always felt like a performance.

Rhythm felt like permission.

He realized: **Flow wasn't a state to achieve — it was a relationship to maintain.**

Like breath

inhale,

exhale,

pause.

---

## From Control to Coexistence

Work hadn't changed.

Deadlines shifted, pressure pulsed, uncertainty stayed a loyal visitor.

But his participation changed.

He no longer tried to silence the noise —

he adjusted his rhythm within it.

A tense call came in; he noticed his jaw tighten, then soften.

An urgent email arrived, he paused before typing, letting breath lead thought.

A last-minute demand landed; he inhaled once, exhaled twice.

Small movements,

Micro-choices.

Tiny recalibrations.

These became his tuning forks for alignment.

He had fought time for years.

Now he walked with it.

The world hadn't slowed.

His panic had.

**Soul-Lag™ Insight:**

***When you stop fighting time, time stops fighting you.***

---

### The Conversation with Meera

During an evening walk, Meera glanced at him.

"You seem… lighter."

He nodded. "I stopped trying to win against life. I started walking with it."

She smiled softly.

"You used to chase meaning."

"And now?" he asked.

"Now it seems meaning is walking beside you."

He chuckled.

A brief sting of the old urgency flickered — the instinct to earn peace.

He caught it.

Let it pass.

"Maybe meaning was always here," he said.

"I was just running too fast to see it."

---

## The Lesson in Movement

During a workshop, someone asked:

"How do you stay in flow when everything collapses again?"

Arnav didn't rush to answer.

He let silence breathe first.

Then he smiled

"You don't. You fall out of flow — and fall back in faster. That's the art."

He sketched waves on the board, saying:

**"Life moves in waves.**

**Don't flatten it —**

**learn to surf it."**

The room stilled.

Some nodded.

Some closed their eyes.

Most simply exhaled — relief unclenching years of internal pressure.

---

### Reflection Box – Pause & Realign

- When do I feel most naturally aligned — not performing, just being?
- What patterns of resistance can I soften instead of break?
- How can everyday actions become conscious movements?

**Soul-Lag™ Insight:**

**Flow isn't peace without motion.**

**It's peace within motion.**

---

## Closing Scene

That night, he wrote:

"Alignment isn't perfection.

It's the art of returning to rhythm each time you forget the tune."

He closed his notebook,

set it gently on the table,

then turned off the light.

Thunder rolled in the distance.

Rain tapped the glass with uneven beats.

Weeks ago, this sound might have unsettled him.

Tonight, he breathed with it.

Even storms, he realized, have a rhythm.

As sleep settled over him, one thought softened into place:

**"The world outside may rush,**

**but the world inside finally flows."**

And just like that,

Soul-Lag was no longer a wound to heal.

It was wisdom learning to breathe.

## Diagram 8 / Chapter 8

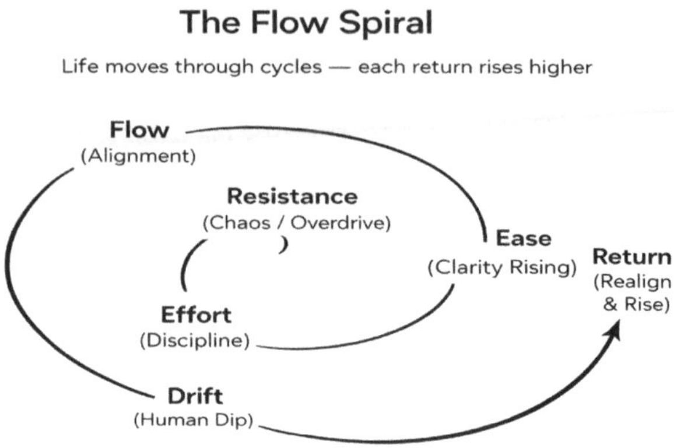




---

*"We spiral, not repeat"*

**– Soul-Lag™ Principle**

---

### Author's Note

*We don't go in circles – we grow in spirals.*

*Each return is wiser than the last.*

CHAPTER 9

# BRIDGING WORLDS

### The Return to Motion

Monday mornings used to feel like collisions.

Today, they felt like choreography.

Arnav still had meetings, deadlines, expectations — the world hadn't slowed for him — but something fundamental had changed:

He no longer divided his life into "spiritual" and "professional," "personal" and "purposeful."

He had stopped living in compartments.

Instead, he began living as one integrated rhythm.

The traffic outside his windows, the inbox filling up, the calendar blocks — none of it felt like an enemy anymore.

A faint tug of old urgency surfaced as he glanced at the clock.

He noticed it,

let it soften.

The world wasn't an assault on his inner peace — it had become his training ground.

---

## The Two Arnavs

Once, he had been two people:

The one the world saw — decisive, articulate, composed.

And the one he met only in silence — uncertain, tender, and searching.

For years, they had lived like strangers sharing the same body.

Now, the two no longer fought for dominance.

They had begun to collaborate.

He noticed that when he was steady inside, the room around him softened.

Decisions came more cleaner.

People listened more fully.

He spoke less, but what he said landed deeper.

Perhaps the world outside is only ever a reflection of the one within.

He wrote in his notebook:

"I don't have two worlds anymore.

I live in one — and I am whole in it."

---

## The Leadership of Stillness

During a major client negotiation, tensions rose.

Voices clipped. Chairs shifted. Ego stirred in the air.

A familiar spark of urgency flickered in his chest —

the instinct to jump in, to prove, to steer.

He felt it, acknowledged it, and released it.

Instead of reaching, he breathed.

He let others speak first.

When he did speak, it was measured — slow, precise, grounded.

The room cooled.

Solutions appeared where argument had stood.

Later his manager said quietly,

"You didn't dominate the room,

You anchored it.

That night, he wrote:

***"Leadership is not direction. It's resonance."***

He wasn't just managing work anymore — he was managing energy.

---

## A Personal Bridge

One evening, on the balcony, he told Meera about his father's watch, the race he ran for years, the quiet he was learning to trust again.

She listened without fixing, without guiding — just present.

"I'm proud of you," she said softly.

"For what?" he asked.

"For learning to stand still without feeling guilty."

A tiny ache rose in him — the old reflex to justify worth.

He breathed; it dissolved.

He smiled.

"I think that's the hardest thing I've ever done."

They sat in silence —

And silence felt full.

---

## Reflection Box – Pause & Realign

- Where do I still live in separation — heart vs work, self vs success?
- Where can I respond from stillness instead of momentum?
- What if success is the world syncing to my inner pace?

**Soul-Lag™ Insight**

***When your actions reflect your awareness,***

***you stop performing — you start resonating.***

---

## Closing Scene

That weekend, Arnav was invited to speak at a university.

He looked at the audience — students, dreamers, young professionals — all restless, eager to win.

He began, not with advice, but with honesty.

"I've lived at both extremes — speed and silence.

Both broke me. Both built me.

What changed my life wasn't slowing down but syncing up."

He paused.

"You'll feel it one day — when your world moves faster than your soul.

That's not failure. That's your signal.

That's **Soul-Lag.**

And that's where real alignment begins."

The auditorium fell silent — the good kind of silence.

He could feel it — resonance.

For the first time, the inner and outer Arnav were not negotiating peace.

They were already one.

---

**Diagram 9 / Chapter 9**

*Inner Balance Cycle*

PRESENCE WITHIN AWARENESS AND ACTION

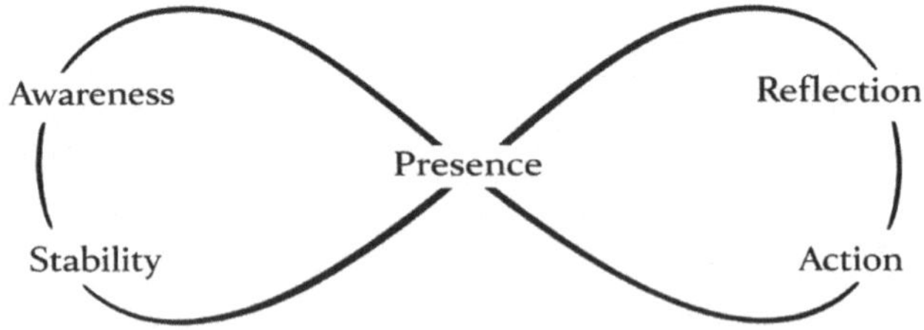

---

*Balance is a comeback game.*

**– Soul-Lag™ Principle**

---

## Author's Note

*Leadership isn't staying balanced —*

*It's returning faster.*

CHAPTER 10

# THE LOOP CONTINUES

## The Circle, Not the Line

Months had passed since Arnav's breath had first tightened in that glass-walled boardroom — the moment everything cracked open.

He had changed cities, changed roles, and changed how he moved through the world — but the biggest shift wasn't external.

It was tempo.

Life hadn't slowed.

He had learned to move differently within it.

Deadlines still rushed, phones still buzzed, the world still sprinted.

Yet beneath it all, he carried rhythm instead of urgency.

His growth had never been linear; he could see that now.

*Every insight had been followed by drift.*

*Every drift, by reflection.*

*Every reflection, by return.*

*Every return, by deeper clarity.*

He smiled, a soft curve of recognition.

Growth wasn't climbing a mountain.

It was orbiting closer to truth, loop by loop.

---

## Morning on the Balcony

Sunday again.

He sipped his tea as sunlight spilled across the railing.

Meera was reading in the corner, peaceful.

He flipped open his notebook — the same one that had followed him through silence, breakdowns, airports, and realignments.

On the first page, his earliest note still read:

**"The lag means I'm alive."**

He smiled softly and wrote below it:

**"And being alive means I keep looping."**

He could now see **Soul-Lag** not as an error, but as a feedback system — a signal that reminded him to realign each time he drifted away from himself.

### The Loop in Motion

Later that week, a strategy review turned tense.

Voices sharpened, timelines collided, ambition pressed against impatience.

Arnav felt the tug —

A pulse quickening, shoulders tightening, the old instinct rising:

fix it fast, assert control, push.

He inhaled

Held

Released

Quietly, inside himself, he traced the familiar path:

**Recognize → Recenter → Reflect → Realign**

He didn't withdraw from the moment — he re-entered it wiser.

When he finally spoke, his voice held clarity, not force.

The room softened.

People heard each other.

Ideas surfaced instead of ego.

Nothing outside had changed —

Only his posture towards the moment.

Awareness had become participation

---

**Reflection Box – Pause & Realign**

- Where am I waiting for peace instead of practicing it?
- What does my drift feel like — in my breath, in my body?
- How can I see repetition not as monotony but as mastery?

**Soul-Lag™ Insight**

***Real growth is looping through awareness with a little more grace each time.***

---

## Closing Scene — The Eternal Return

Evening.

A walk by the river — the same river he had once reached in exhaustion and desperate for stillness.

The skyline glittered.

Traffic hummed.

Life moved.

So did he — but with it, not against it.

He stopped at the water's edge, watching ripples carry moonlight.

"I don't want stillness to last forever," he whispered.

"I want rhythm to never stop."

The soul never asked for silence from life — only harmony within it.

Soul-Lag wasn't escape.

It was an invitation.

A pulse.

A whisper.

A returning.

He breathed in the night air — cool, steady.

The moon rose slowly, reflected perfectly in the rippling water.

One image above, one below — yet both the same.

He took a deep breath, smiled, and walked on.

And the loop continued.

---

## Diagram 10 / Chapter 10

DUAL-WORLD CONVERGENCE

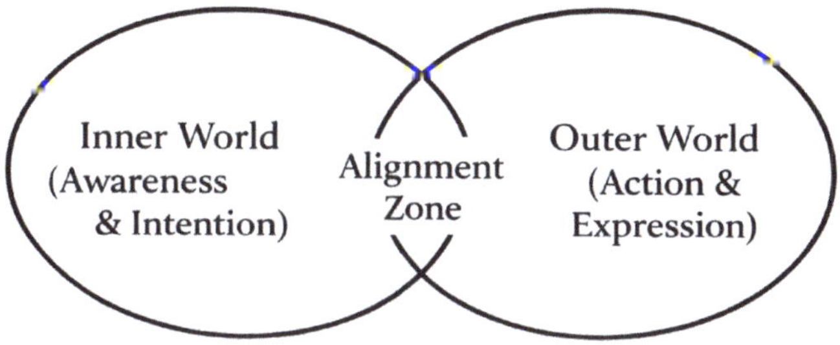


*"Peace is participation without distortion."*



---

*"The alignment zone is where inner peace becomes outer impact."*

**– Soul-Lag™ Principle**

---

### Author's Note

*Alignment is inner peace in motion — felt inside, seen outside.*

# EPILOGUE – THE ALIGNMENT WITHIN

## The Return to Self

The night was quiet — not the forced quiet of noise-cancelling headphones, but the kind that hums from the inside out.

Arnav sat at his desk, the window half open, the wind carrying the scent of rain and distant earth.

The same city that once overwhelmed him now felt alive in harmony.

He thought of the journey: the burnout, the silence, the drift, the rediscovery.

Nothing dramatic had happened outside.

But everything had changed within.

He realized that transformation doesn't announce itself —

it unfolds quietly, one awareness at a time.

He flipped open his notebook to the last page and wrote:

"**Soul-Lag** is not a problem to solve.

It's the language through which the soul speaks.

Every drift is a message. Every pause, an answer."

He paused, smiled, and underlined one final phrase:

"The alignment was never outside — it was always within."

## Epilogue / Diagram

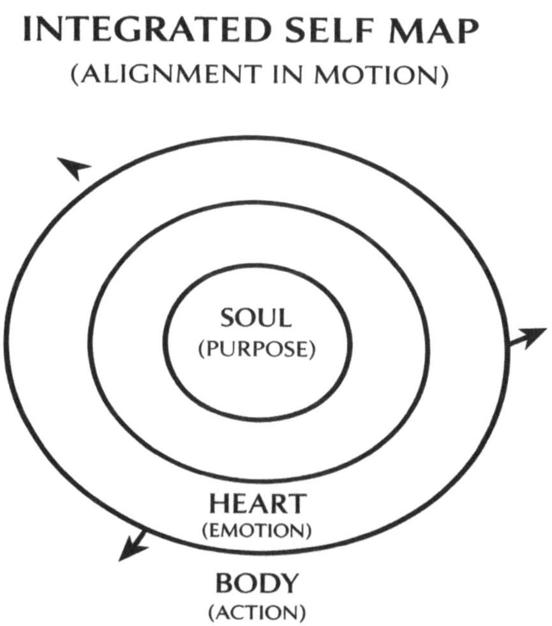

*"The soul whispers, the heart responds, the body becomes."*

**– Soul-Lag™ Principle**

## Author's Note

*We change from the inside out — soul to heart to action.*

*The soul begins, the heart aligns, the body expresses.*

*Alignment isn't forced — it unfolds from within.*

# BONUS CHAPTER

## The Return Before the Rise

When knowing outruns becoming

There are moments in life when our mind races ahead of our inner world.

When we know better…

but cannot yet live better.

Not because we are weak.

But because we are human, and repair takes time.

I call that space Soul-Lag —

the gap between realizing who you want to be

and having the inner capacity to be that person.

Soul-Lag isn't failure.

It's the psyche catching up.

It's strength resting so it can return.

Many high achievers don't burn out because they lack discipline —

they burn out because they use discipline against themselves.

They move before they were ready inside.

They force where they need to recover.

They push where they need to listen.

And yet… they survived.

You survived.

And that deserves respect, not regret.

---

## Why knowing isn't enough

Insight is obvious in hindsight.

Capacity is only clear in the moment.

You can have clarity and still feel unable to act.

That doesn't mean you are stuck —

it means you are preparing.

Real growth doesn't begin when you realize the truth.

It begins when you can hold the truth without collapsing into old habits.

Growth is not intellectual first —

it is emotional and energetic first.

---

## The natural order of change

Before behaviour changes, something quieter happens:

I understand.

I accept.

I feel safe enough to try.

I take one small step.

I repeat.

When we try to rush that sequence, we don't fail —

we simply overextend.

Change is not a leap.

It is a steady step repeated until it becomes who you are.

---

## Start where you can stay

Most people start big because they want fast results.

But big beginnings often break under their own weight.

True transformation begins small —

not out of fear,

but out of respect for your nervous system and your humanity.

The right first step is not the impressive one —

it's the one you can return to tomorrow.

Call it an **Aligned Micro-Step™**—

a tiny action you can do without pressure, shame, or self-abandonment.

Not "small to be safe."

Small to be sustainable.

Start where you can stay.

That is maturity.

That is strength.

That is how lives change quietly and permanently.

---

## The return rhythm

Every meaningful comeback follows a rhythm:

**Pause → Return to yourself → Take one honest step**

Not to prove anything.

Not to catch up.

Simply to live without losing yourself again.

There is no glory in speed if you can't stay there.

There is profound power in steady becoming.

This time, you rise differently —

without leaving yourself behind.

---

## If you struggled before — honour that

If you tried to change and fell back, it's not because you lacked will.

It's because your system needed space, repair, and gentleness.

Self-blame slows growth.

Self-respect accelerates it.

You didn't break.

You paused so you could return stronger, softer, and truer.

That pause was wisdom, not weakness.

---

## A simple re-entry guide

Each morning, ask yourself:

- What matters to me right now?
- What can I do today without force?
- How can I stay with myself while doing it?

Each evening, finish with one line:

Today I respected myself by…

That's enough.

Change loves consistency, not drama.

---

## Closing

The world tells you to move fast.

Soul-Lag asks you to return first.

Return to presence.

Return to breath.

Return to dignity.

Return to yourself.

And then move —

not because you're chasing life,

but because you are ready to live it well.

You haven't fallen behind.

You've been gathering yourself.

This time, you rise with yourself, not away from yourself.

And that rise lasts.

## Soul-Lag Reflection Workbook

Gentle structure for a steady return

This workbook is not for pushing.

It is for **coming back to yourself**, slowly and honestly.

Small pages, big honesty.

---

**1) Where am I right now?**

Complete these prompts softly

No judgment — just noticing.

What part of me is tired?

---

What part of me is ready?

---

Where did I abandon myself in the past?

---

Where am I learning to stay with myself now?

---

**2) A check-in with myself**

Rate, 1–5 (quiet honesty)

| Reflection | 1 | 2 | 3 | 4 | 5 |
|---|---|---|---|---|---|
| I understand why I slowed down | ○ | ○ | ○ | ○ | ○ |

| Reflection | 1 | 2 | 3 | 4 | 5 |
|---|---|---|---|---|---|
| I am not blaming myself for needing rest | ○ | ○ | ○ | ○ | ○ |
| I feel safe taking life slowly right now | ○ | ○ | ○ | ○ | ○ |
| I am ready to take small steps again | ○ | ○ | ○ | ○ | ○ |
| I trust gradual growth | ○ | ○ | ○ | ○ | ○ |

### 3) My Aligned Micro-step

Start where you can stay.

No heroics, no proving.

Just one honest step.

Today, one small action I can sustain is:

______________________________________________

Why this feels possible:

______________________________________________

______________________________________________

### 4) How I will support myself

What helps me feel calm before I act?

(Examples: breath, stillness, stretching, silence)

---

What helps me stay gentle if I slip?

(Examples: pause, walk, truth, rest, kindness)

---

### 5) Evening return line

Write one line each night:

Today, I respected myself by…

---

That's enough.

That's the work.

---

### 6) Weekly grounding check

Once a week, ask:

Did I stay with myself?

Did I move slowly enough to breathe?

Did I honour my energy instead of forcing?

Did I take small steps instead of dramatic ones?

And then write:

One thing I want to continue:

______________________________________________

One thing I will soften next week:

______________________________________________

______________________________________________

**Quiet reminders**

- You don't have to hurry to rebuild.
- Slow steps are still steps.
- Rest is preparation.
- Your pace is not a problem — it is a message.
- Self-respect is the foundation, not the reward.

**Mantra for this season**

Return.
Move gently.
Stay with yourself.
No rush.
No noise.

Just presence and small good steps.

# BEFORE YOU BEGIN: LISTENING FOR THE LAG — YOUR INNER REMINDER TO REALIGN

***"Soul-Lag isn't a problem to fix; it's a signal to feel.*** *It's life's quiet tap on the shoulder — asking you to slow down enough to arrive."*

We all drift.

The mind races, the calendar fills faster than the heart can follow, and achievement outruns meaning.

That space between outer pace and inner rhythm is **Soul-Lag** — not a fault, but feedback.

To notice your lag is to notice life.

Each signal below is an *invitation* to return to rhythm.

| Everyday Situation | What It's Whispering | A Simple Way to Realign |
|---|---|---|
| **Work & Ambition** – Doing more, feeling flat. | "Your purpose hasn't caught up with your performance." | Pause and remember why you began, not what you are doing. |
| **Relationships** – Surrounded yet unseen. | "Presence is missing from connection." | Listen without multitasking. Feel before you fix. |
| **Body & Energy** – Tired even after rest. | "The body is carrying un-expressed stories." | One conscious breath between tasks, not just at the end. |
| **Time & Routine** – Always rushing, never arriving. | "You've lost rhythm with time." | Mark moments—morning, meal, meeting—with a single conscious breath. |
| **Emotion & Expression** – Quick irritation, quiet joy. | "Emotion wants to move, not be managed." | Name the feeling; it softens immediately. |

| Everyday Situation | What It's Whispering | A Simple Way to Realign |
|---|---|---|
| **Purpose & Growth** – Restlessness after success. | "Meaning needs a turn to speak." | Let silence decide the next goal. |
| **Community & World** – Constant input, little inspiration. | "You're connected, not nourished." | Choose depth over noise once a day. |

*The lag isn't punishment—it's presence calling you home.*

# CORE MESSAGE OF SOUL-LAG

**Soul-Lag is the loving distance between what you're doing and what you're truly feeling.**

It appears whenever:

- achievement outruns awareness
- Productivity replaces presence
- Speed replaces rhythm

You don't eliminate lag.

You **listen** to it.

Each signal is an invitation:

*Pause, Breathe, Return*

---

# KEY SYMPTOMS OF SOUL-LAG (ACROSS LIFE DIMENSIONS)

| Life Dimension | Gentle Signal | What It's Really Asking For |
|---|---|---|
| **Mind** | Racing thoughts, clarity thin. | Space between ideas. |
| **Body** | Fatigue without cause. | Movement to feel, not measures. |
| **Heart** | Irritability or numbness. | Honest emotional expression. |
| **Time** | Rushing past joy. | Rituals that shape the day. |
| **Work** | Success feels hollow. | Purpose and rest built into progress. |

| Life Dimension | Gentle Signal | What It's Really Asking For |
|---|---|---|
| **Relationships** | Saying much, feeling little. | Presence before response. |
| **Creativity** | Busy but uninspiring. | Silence for imagination |
| **Spiritual** | Calm outside, Noise inside. | Simple acts of stillness—breath, gratitude, solitude. |

# SOUL-LAG GLOSSARY

| Term | Meaning |
|---|---|
| **Soul-Lag** | The natural gap between outer speed and inner rhythm—a gentle reminder to realign. |
| **Alignment Loop** | The living cycle of *Recognize →Recenter → Reflect→ Realign.* |
| **Listening for the Lag** | The practice of noticing subtle signals before imbalance grows. |
| **Flow Continuum** | The curve that shows how real flow arises when effort meets ease. |
| **Drift** | Temporary disconnection; not failure, but feedback. |
| **Reflection Box – Pause & Realign** | End-of-chapter pauses that turn insight into gentle action. |
| **Heart–Mind–Body Sync** | Inner integration: when thought, emotion, and action move in harmony. |

| Term | Meaning |
|---|---|
| **Flow Window** | The personal zone where energy and attention align naturally. |
| **Bridge of Worlds** | The meeting point between inner clarity and outer responsibility. |
| **Alignment Spiral** | Lifelong rhythm of awareness returning at deeper levels. It helps in evolution |
| **Realignment** | Returning to one's natural rhythm after drift; the act of conscious correction without judgment. |
| **Presence** | Arriving fully where you already are. |
| **Aligned Micro-Step** | A small, sincere action with alignment |

## Closing Reflection Box – Pause & Realign

1 ☐When did life whisper "slow down," — and you mistook it for stress?

2 ☐Which Soul-Lag signal visits you most often — and what might it be teaching you?

3 ☐What gentle act can help you return — not force you forward?

*The world won't slow down.*

*But you can always return to rhythm.*

## Soul-Lag Workbook — Find Your Rhythm Again

---

### 1. The Soul-Lag Alignment Scan

Purpose: Notice where speed is outrunning soul.

| Area | Outer Speed (1-10) | Inner Alignment (1-10) | Emotion in 5 Words | One Gentle Adjustment |
|---|---|---|---|---|
| Work / Ambition | | | | |
| Relationships | | | | |
| Health / Energy | | | | |
| Purpose / Meaning | | | | |
| Creativity / Learning | | | | |

Reflection Prompts

- Where am I moving fast but feeling thin or hollow?
- Where am I performing instead of participating?
- What area needs a pause, not pressure?

Note: Don't fix — notice first, name later.

---

## 2. Map Your Alignment Loop

Purpose: Practice Arnav's cycle consciously.

Draw:

Recognize → Recenter → Reflect → Realign

Then answer:

| Loop Phase | Your Answer |
|---|---|
| Recognize — What truth surfaced? | |
| Recenter — Breath / grounding I used | |
| Reflect — What was real vs fear? | |
| Realign — What will I do differently? | |

Add a "Breath Moment"

4-2-6 breath: Inhale 4, hold 2, exhale 6 → signal safety.

Mantra:

"I return gently. I move wisely."

---

### 3. Drift Journal

Purpose: Turn relapse into information, not shame.

For 7 days:

| Moment I Drifted- | Trigger - | My Reaction | -My Return | Lesson / Pattern |
|---|---|---|---|---|
| | | | | |

Guidance

- Drift = notification from the soul
- Focus on shortening return time not avoiding drift

"I don't fall behind — I find my way back."

---

### 4. Flow Window Audit

Purpose: Find your natural performance rhythm.

| Energizes Me (Flow) | Drains Me (Friction) |
|---|---|
| | |

Questions

- When do I naturally think best?
- Who drains vs nourishes me?
- 1 shift to increase flow by 10%?

Identity Reminder

"I don't chase time. I choose tempo."

---

## 5. Bridge Inner & Outer Worlds

Purpose: Integrate being + doing.

| **Inner Intention** | **Outer Expression** |
|---|---|
| Presence | Slow speech. Eye contact. Pause. |
| Calm | 30-sec breath before react. |
| Self-worth | Work from clarity, not proving. |
| Creativity | 1 hour weekly exploration. |

Question: Where am I still negotiating between worlds?

---

## 6. Daily Alignment Ritual

Purpose: 3-minute end-of-day reset

| Prompt | Response |
|---|---|
| What drained me? | |
| What nourished me? | |
| Where did I drift? | |
| How did I return? | |
| One intention for tomorrow | |

Evening closing line

"I release proving. I return to being."

---

### 7. The Alignment Spiral

Place on your final page:

Awareness → Recenter → Reflect → Realign → Flow → Drift → Awareness

Every loop = higher intelligence, softer edges, deeper truth

The world won't slow down.

You will learn to move within it without losing yourself.

Every time you move through it, you don't repeat the past — you *elevate it.*

*The world won't slow down. But you can always return to rhythm.*

✅ End of Workbook — "Your Realignment Journey"

# CLOSING NOTE TO THE READER

If you've come this far, you've already begun your realignment.

Soul-Lag isn't a pause from life; it's your soul asking for participation.

Every exercise, every silence, every realization brings you closer to the self you left waiting somewhere along the way.

So take the next breath — consciously.

The loop continues, and now, it's yours.

# THE LETTER TO THE READER

He looked out the window, thinking of everyone like him — running, striving, chasing.

He thought of students burning with ambition, mothers juggling unseen battles, and leaders carrying silent exhaustion.

He wanted to reach each one and say:

"You are not broken because you're tired.

You're tired because your life has outpaced your soul.

And that's not weakness — it's wisdom calling you home."

He closed his eyes and whispered softly:

"Don't escape the lag. Listen to it.

That's where your alignment begins."

**The Realization**

The next morning, he woke with no rush.

The sun rose, steady and golden.

Meera handed him a coffee.

She asked, "So, what's next?"

He smiled. "Whatever aligns."

### Final Reflection Box – Pause & Realign

- What part of me is asking to slow — not stop — but sync?
- Which actions of mine no longer match my inner truth?
- What would life look like if every moment became a loop of awareness, action, and reflection?

The world will always move fast.

The art is not to slow it down — but to stay in step with your soul.

# CLOSING LINE

He placed the cup on the table, looked out at the morning sky, and breathed deeply.

The horizon shimmered softly — not an ending, not a beginning, but a loop continuing beyond sight.

Soul-Lag™ was never a pause in his story.

It was the story itself.

# ABOUT THE AUTHOR

Gaurav Patel is a corporate leader turned author, storyteller, and thinker who has spent over two decades navigating the demanding world of business, leadership, and transformation.

His professional journey — spanning high-pressure environments, constant reinvention, and human complexity — offered him an unfiltered view of modern success and the silent fatigue that often comes with it.

Driven by his own search for balance between ambition and awareness, Gaurav developed the Soul-Lag™ framework — a philosophy that helps individuals and organizations reconnect with rhythm, reflection, and realignment.

His approach blends real-world pragmatism with emotional intelligence, making his work relatable to professionals, creators, students, and seekers alike.

Through his writing , Gaurav helps people transform exhaustion into evolution — not by slowing down, but by syncing up.

When he's not writing or speaking, he can be found exploring quiet spaces, sketching ideas for new models of inner growth, or simply watching the world move — slower, but with purpose.

Soul-Lag™: Realigning Your Life is his first book — and the beginning of a movement toward mindful momentum in an accelerating world.

# ACKNOWLEDGMENTS

No journey of alignment happens alone.

This book, too, is a weaving of many hearts, minds, and moments.

To my parents, whose quiet sacrifices built the foundation I stand on, and to my wife, for holding space when words ran out — your patience fills every pause in these pages. Thank you for being my constant anchor through every phase of drift and discovery.

To my son, **Rivyan** — you are the truest reminder of rhythm. Your laughter, your curiosity, your effortless presence — they keep teaching me what alignment really means.

This book is, in many ways, a reflection of what I hope you'll always carry within you: balance, awareness, and the courage to pause.

To the friends and mentors who questioned, challenged, and reflected — your insights became my realignments.

To my colleagues and teams across years of corporate life — thank you for the lessons hidden in pressure and the humanity found within performance.

To the readers — thank you for picking up this book.

Whether you found it in fatigue, curiosity, or quiet hope, I wrote it for you.

If even one page helps you breathe easier or see yourself with more compassion, then Soul-Lag™ has done its work.

And finally, to the rhythm that never stopped — the heartbeat beneath the noise — thank you for waiting until I could listen.